CW01022701

THE SPIRIT OF

DEVON

LEE PENGELLY

HALSGROVE

First published in Great Britain in 2007

Copyright text and photographs © 2007 Lee Pengelly

British Library Cataloguing-in-Publication Data
A CIP record for this title is available from the British Library

ISBN 978 1 84114 656 0

HALSGROVE
Halsgrove House
Ryelands   Farm Industrial Estate
Bagley Green, Wellington
Somerset TA21 9PZ
Tel: 01823 653777
Fax: 01823 216796
email: sales@halsgrove.com
website: www.halsgrove.com

Printed and bound by D'Auria Industrie Grafiche Spa, Italy

Introduction

Devon is undoubtedly the most beautiful county in England, or so Devonians would have us believe. Even putting local pride aside, few would dispute that the county has so many scenic delights to offer that rhyming Devon with Heaven trips naturally off the tongue.

In this book Lee Pengelly captures the spirit of the county through his marvellous photographs giving each of us a chance to take home a little piece of Heaven – that is Devon – as a permanent memento.

Moored boats on the River Tamar at Plymouth.

The Victorian pier at Paignton silhouetted against a red dawn sky.

View from the cliff railway that has linked the 'twin villages' of Lynton and Lynmouth since their Victorian heyday.

Opposite page: Lynmouth sea front sits below high cliffs, at the mercy of the East and West Lyn rivers which meet here.

The picturesque harbour at Clovelly

Opposite page:
Heather clad cliffs overlooking the Bristol Channel
on the North Devon coast at Lynton

The Esplanade at Exmouth, deserted under dramatic skies but usually a popular tourist spot with its wide sandy beach.

Opposite page:
Dusk light illuminates the sky and sea at Westcombe beach.

Cockwood Harbour,
near Starcross.

Opposite page:
Rickety fencing snaking
through protected sand
dunes at Bantham.

Dramatic sunset at Hope Cove.

An old ladder becomes
part of the landscape
on Dawlish Warren.

Warm evening sunlight lights up the old Fort at
Bovisand at the mouth of Plymouth Sound.

Opposite page:
Dawn light on the River Tamar at Plymouth.

Firework display over
Plymouth Sound.

Opposite page:
The Tamar road bridge and
Brunel's railway bridge.
The Royal Albert Bridge was
Isambard Kingdom Brunel's
last great achievement,
spanning the River Tamar.

Smeaton's Tower, Plymouth's well-known landmark, was once the Eddystone Lighthouse and took up its home on the Hoe in 1882.

Opposite page:
The Exeter Canal at Haven Banks.

Drake's Circus shopping centre, Plymouth.

The unusual sails of Plymouth's Sainsburys supermarket
set against a purple dusk sky.

The attractive town of Bideford sits alongside the River Torridge, spanned by a stout 24-arch bridge dating back to the fourteenth century.

Opposite page: Twinkling lights of Torbay at night.

Cottages at Cockington, Torquay's traditional village within a town.

Opposite page:
Dawn mist encircles the church at Modbury.

Every spring time vibrant clusters of daffodils emerge adding a touch of colour to South Molton's parish church green.

Opposite page:
Boats moored on the River Yealm at Newton Ferrers.

Cathedral Close, Exeter.

Opposite page:
The early-twentieth-century Britannia
Royal Naval College at Dartmouth makes a fine
and imposing backdrop to the harbour below.

No trip to Exeter would be complete without seeing the cathedral,
one of the finest in the country with its twin Norman towers,
magnificent three-storey West Front with well-preserved statues.

Haldon Belvedere, Dunchideock. This fine folly was built in
1788 as a memorial to Major General Stringer Lawrence.

The setting sun highlights the
simple lines of St Helena
Church on Lundy.

Opposite page:
Coldharbour Mill, Uffculme,
a wool mill until 1981,
now a working museum.

The fourteenth-century Rising Sun Hotel on Lynmouth's
harbourside was once a haunt popular with smugglers.

The last rays of the sun gently light up this crop
of oilseed rape above Wembury village.

Mute swan enjoying the
calm waters of a leat
near Tiverton.

Opposite page:
An old oak tree on the banks
of the River Erme.

Rowing boats moored among the reed beds at Slapton Ley, the largest natural freshwater lake in Devon and an important haven for bird life.

A buttercup-filled meadow at Creacombe, Yealmpton.

Though Burrator Reservoir on Dartmoor's western fringe is
a popular tourist spot, solitude can still be found nearby.

Opposite page: A misty morning at Umberleigh in the Taw Valley, near South Molton.

Sunflowers adorn a field near Exeter.

A wintry scene on the edge of the moors near
Okehampton; snowfall comes and goes within days.

Maize crop at
Rix Farm, Tiverton.

Opposite page:
Low autumnal light illuminates
this solitary tree overlooking
Sheepstor village.

A fisherman on the River Dart.

Opposite page:
Clapper bridge at Postbridge. The best known bridge of this type,
spanning the East Dart river, it is the largest clapper on the moor at
over 40 feet in length. The newer road bridge stands alongside.

Powder Mills at Postbridge. The remains of a gunpowder
factory opened in 1844 by George Frean.

Opposite page:
A rainbow appears over the church
at Widecombe-in-the-Moor.

Leather Tor, Dartmoor

Opposite page:
Purple heather at its best
beside the Warren House Inn
at Headland Warren.

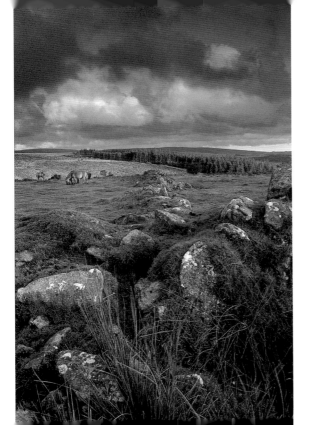

Dartmoor ponies graze
near Princetown.

Opposite page:
A wind-battered tree bathed
in moonlight at Sheepstor.

55

Brent Tor church sits atop a 1130ft-high volcanic outcrop near Tavistock.

Princetown church tower stands like a beacon in the bleak landscape.

Merrivale stone row.

Opposite page:
The River Dart at Dartmeet.

Wheal Betsy near Tavistock
was worked for tin periodically
in the nineteenth century until
1870. The disused engine house is
now owned by the National Trust.

Bennett's Cross overlooking Headland Warren near Postbridge. The medieval cross marked an ancient track over the moor.

The unpredictable Dartmoor weather can change from glorious sunshine to violent storms in a matter of hours.

Dartmoor ponies grazing near Black Tor on Dartmoor.

Silhouette of Leeden Tor against the evening sky.